Relationships

Helen Adams Garrett

ISBN-10: 0-86690-621-5
ISBN-13: 978-0-86690-621-0

Cover Design: Jack Cipolla

Published by:
American Federation of Astrologers, Inc.
6535 S. Rural Road
Tempe AZ 85283.

www.astrologers.com

Printed in the United States of America

Contents

Books by Helen Adams Garrett

Understanding Retrogrades

More About Retrogrades

Unlocking Interceptions

Karma in the Horoscope

Interpret Horoscopes in 24 Steps

Health in the Horoscope

Chapter 1

Your Ideal Companion

A companion is someone who is desirable company. The ideal companion is someone who is desirable under all circumstances. In a romantic sense, we immediately classify the ideal companion as a lover.

Every person you know is represented by one of the houses of your horoscope. The seventh house represents other people in general, the marriage partner in particular and coworkers or business partners.

As a rule, the seventh house progressions and transits show the current activity between self and relationships. The first marriage partner is described in character and type by the seventh house. The second marriage partner is described in character and type by the ninth house, but activity of that marriage is still governed by the seventh house. You might say it is the same stage and show with a different lead role. The third marriage stars the eleventh house character and type. The fourth partner is so much like the individual because he or she is represented by the first house, that the marriage is usually of short duration. They are too much alike to get along.

The fifth partner identifies with the traits depicted by the third house, and so on around the chart. Regardless of the identifying type as described by the respective houses, the events of relationships are still read from the seventh house.

Chapter 2

What Is a Type?

The Sun sign reflects twenty-five percent or less of who we are. If the Sun is afflicted, stands alone in a sign or is in the twelfth house, its qualities might not be obvious. An afflicted Sun can lose some of its power, and one that stands alone might get little reinforcement from its sign. The Sun in the twelfth house can be so withdrawn as to be unidentifiable by the Sun's traits.

A person can be one type socially, another in the work world and still another in the family. Only a few people are the same in all areas. Someone who comes on strong to you may go completely unnoticed by someone else.

Identifying Types
1. Sun sign
2. Moon sign
3. Ascending sign

4. Stellium in a sign (a group of planets in a sign)
5. Stellium in a house (a group of planets in a house)
6. Planet in the first house
7. Most elevated planet (closest to the Midheaven)
8. Planet conjunct the Sun

Planetary Examples of Types

- Sun + Moon in Cancer = Leo type
- Sun + Moon in Leo = Cancer type
- Sun + Moon in any sign = Cancer or Leo type
- Moon conjunct Ascendant = Cancer type
- Sun conjunct Ascendant = Leo type
- Sun in twelfth house = Pisces type
- Venus conjunct Sun = Taurus or Libra type
- Mars conjunct Sun = Aries type
- Mars conjunct Moon = Cancer or Aries type
- Jupiter conjunct Sun or Ascendant = Sagittarius type
- Jupiter conjunct Moon = Sagittarius, Cancer or Pisces type
- Saturn conjunct Sun or Ascendant = Capricorn type
- Saturn conjunct Moon = Cancer type
- Uranus conjunct Sun, Moon or Ascendant = Aquarius type
- Neptune conjunct Sun, Moon or Ascendant = Pisces type
- Pluto conjunct Sun, Moon or Ascendant = Scorpio type

Every person is something like his or her Sun sign. You might align with one who has the same ascending sign as your Sun. You are very likely at some time in your life to have a romance or affair with someone whose Sun is in the sign of your fifth house of romance, love and affairs. Remember also to consider the fifth sign from the Sun, which is the solar fifth house and equates to your ideas of romance. We tend to seek opposites as companions, but those with familiarity also attract.

When analyzing types, consider the eight points above. Following is an actual example of how type works:

A Leo man with Scorpio rising married a Taurus Sun person. Her Taurus Sun fell in his seventh house of partners. Her Pisces elements were in his fifth house with no strong bonds, nor was her eighth house compatible. Love went away early.

His next relationship was with a Scorpio Sun with a Virgo Ascendant. Her Neptune is on her Ascendant and rules his fifth house, Pisces. He seeks Neptunian types for romance, and her first house Neptune makes her much like a Pisces.

Her Scorpio Sun is a reflection of him because he has Scorpio rising. Her Venus in Scorpio conjunct her Sun (point 8) identifies with her Venusian qualities to satisfy his seventh house Taurus and complement his Scorpio Ascendant.

As a Leo Sun, Pisces falls eight signs away (sex angle), and with Neptune in the first house, her Pisces type satisfies his eighth house. Since she has Neptune in Virgo and Venus and Sun in Scorpio, the Virgo ascendant is not puritanical and supplies ample romance for his Leo Sun.

The Taurus wife had been more interested in love of money than love of love, which was unsatisfactory to romantic Leo with sexy Scorpio rising.

Another example:

He has a Cancer Ascendant, but an interception causes Libra to fall on his fifth house of romance. She has a Libra ascendant. He has Capricorn on the seventh house and she has Saturn near her Ascendant. She also has tenth house planets and is Capricornian in many ways. He has Aquarius on the eighth house and she is Uranian, probably because Uranus aspects six planets in her chart and is the point of a yod.

His Sun in Aquarius puts Gemini five signs from his Sun. She has a Gemini Moon. Leo opposes his Sun sign, representing partnerships. In many respects she is like Leo because of a stellium in her Sun sign.

Reversing the comparison:

Her Libra Ascendant displays his Sun sign, Aquarius, on her fifth house of romance. She has Aries on the seventh. His Sun is conjunct Mars, ruler of Aries.

She has Taurus on the eighth house, and his Saturn in the first house in Cancer is gentle and protective to fill the required qualities of Taurus.

Her Sun in Cancer opposes Capricorn, where he has two planets, and Saturn in his first house causes him to be Capricornian by type. The fifth sign from her Sun is Scorpio. He has three strong planets in his eighth house, giving Scorpio traits and type. The eighth sign from her Sun is Aquarius, his Sun.

The eighth house (eighth sign) from the Sun is very frequently the Sun or Moon sign of the sex partner. The type is in some way represented there, provided the sex partner is selected by the individual and not chosen by others, as is the custom in some nations.

When two people become acquainted and grow close until there is a magnet between them and sex is allowed, the relationship stands a good chance of being beneficial. But it is the trend to meet and hop immediately in bed, followed by one or the other moving in. It is not difficult to get someone to move in when he or she is looking for a place to live. Then the eighth house instantly takes its additional energy—joint possessions. The two are not well acquainted and it comes as a surprise when she learns his pet is a boa constrictor, and he discovers she does not do dishes, cook or clean and, since it is expensive, limits the house cleaning service to once a month.

When she hangs on tighter than the boa constrictor, he becomes confused as to which to separate from. She soon finds herself frightened and the victim of his anger. It ends when they are sharing an intimate moment and the boa snuggles around them.

If the friendship bonds are exceptionally strong, less romance and sex may be no problem. When friendship bonds are weak and sex is strong, a separation in attitudes may occur when passion wanes because of age, illness or difficulties.

Chapter 3

Romance

The fifth house shows what that person enjoys in the form of entertainment, pleasure and hobby interests. The fifth house is recognized as the house of romance and true love. Romance and courtship precede marriage, and if there is conflict between the character and type described by the fifth house person and the seventh house qualities, romance may fade soon after marriage.

For example, one may be slow, patient and easygoing in courtship and the spouse finds after marriage that the partner awakens early and creates a stir of activity, much of it noisy and annoying. What had been seen as slow, patient and easygoing was actually a result of fatigue or deliberate charm.

The important thing is that the fifth house tells what the individual enjoys. The husband or wife should show evidence by type of having qualities applicable to the energies of the fifth house, for pleasure, and the seventh house, to complement qualities of self in order to be an appropriate partner.

It is important to enjoy some of the same things—TV, sports, gardening, music, travel, cooking, bicycling, group activity, dancing. These are some positive shared pleasures. Some negative pleasures which deteriorate in a relationship are eating out, bar hopping, shopping, doing nothing and sex only.

Fifth House

The fifth house is romantic affairs. It is said that one whose fifth house ruler is in the first house has many affairs. Certainly everyone does not have that. You may never have but one romance, but you still want to know where to start looking for it. What type will it be?

Aries on the fifth house cusp (Sagittarius Ascendant) attracts the independent type who pops in and out, is ambitious and wants to be ahead of the stream in the ticket line.

Taurus on the fifth house cusp (Capricorn Ascendant) may help to explain why Capricorn gets a late start. The Taurus fifth both seeks and attracts money and material values. Taurus is slow to arrive and long to stay.

Gemini on the fifth house cusp (Aquarius Ascendant) provides the need for changeability in a dual personality type or with more than one at a time. Could we speculate that means more than one friend and in love with all of them?

Cancer on the fifth house cusp (Pisces Ascendant) attracts the homemaker. The ultimate goal is to establish its own school of fish and have a home and family.

Leo on the fifth house cusp signals a bold Aries Ascendant who seeks true love (Leo). The Aries desire to be first is filled by Leo leadership.

Virgo on the fifth house cusp (Taurus Ascendant) seeks one who is practical and enjoys luxuries, as well as a padded pocket. In entertainment, Virgo chooses just the right amount of whatever and in good taste without overexertion—the money counter.

Libra on the fifth house cusp (Gemini Ascendant) attracts balance. Gemini means two of everything; so in romance often asks "Which one do I really love?" Once the decision is made—beautiful!

Scorpio on the fifth house cusp attracts sexy types. After all, the underlying need to every Cancer Ascendant is to become a parent. (Cancer women need children —her man is usually one of them. Cancer men tend to want to be the only child of the partner, if not the baby of his own family.) Scorpio desires to procreate and needs to be understood without prying.

Sagittarius on the fifth house cusp attracts many affairs. Leo, the lover, is likely on the Ascendant. Sagittarius, the gift giver, is flamboyant in entertainment. Sports fans, foreigners and distant travel are of interest.

Capricorn on the fifth house cusp (Virgo Ascendant) attracts big business types of a serious nature who are often older. Capricorn practicality comes in many forms other than a Capricorn Sun, but one thing certain is that entertainment and romantic contacts must have value.

Aquarius on the fifth house cusp usually belongs to a Libra Ascendant. Romance must be interesting and exciting, and entertainment is impulsive and unusual. Libra attracts various types and any one must be unique or the Aquarius fifth house cusp will resort to multiplicity for variety.

Pisces on the fifth house cusp (Scorpio Ascendant) is psychoanalytical or metaphysical, trying to break through to the inner self. Both signs are mysterious in nature and spiritual in attitude. For the two sexiest signs of the zodiac, intrigue is the keyword.

Chapter 4

Partners

The partner may be a multiplicity of people. The seventh house of partnerships represents people with whom we cooperate. They are individuals who supply the missing element of self.

A partnership must be a sharing situation. It may be the person who rides the other horse in the round-up on the range or the one who pays part of the utility bills.

A partner may be the other half of a business relationship or someone who carries the load on the other end of a couch during a move.

Partners share knowledge. One helps both pass science tests, while the other supplies the tips for grades in grammar.

A child's parents, at least for one brief moment, were partners. The husband or wife is a partner. Beds are shared by partners, legal or otherwise. The mere fact that one bed is shared constitutes a partnership.

Cooperative effort is the ideal ingredient for an ideal partner. The seventh house of the horoscope is the indicator of types of people we attract to ourselves in order to complete the missing elements of self. If we find ourselves too frequently dissatisfied with a partner it may be well to analyze what lessons can be learned from the associations we allow to exist.

One who is mistreated by others needs to realize that there is a subconscious desire to be punished or disciplined. Kindness comes to those who seek it.

Seventh House

The seventh house describes partners in general, the first partner in particular. Although, the ninth house might be a clue to the personality or profession of the second partner, the eleventh, the third, etc., the basic quality of the seventh house will follow them all. More detail of these descriptions can be found by examining the ruler of the seventh and the ruler of the ninth, eleventh, etc.

Things go nicely in romance as long as the fifth house is being fulfilled. What happens when marriage results? Adjustments are made. Each partner changes roles and now must, for cooperative results, adjust to the type of relationship described by the seventh house. A major adjustment is that what was "mine" is now "ours." Another major adjustment is the invasion of privacy and having to respond when asked "What are you thinking about?" The seventh house is complimentary to the first and must possess some missing qualities of the self to be satisfying to the individual. But getting too much of what we seek in a five-minute matrimonial ceremony is overwhelming for most of us.

It is much easier to be in a fifth house affair than to be in a seventh house partnership. In romance we seek pleasure, which can have some diversion and substitution. In a seventh house partnership, we are stuck with a commitment which not only involves self but all we own. It certainly does not help matters if we think we own the other person. We have possession only to their commitment, and we share their body. Share—that's it!

Chapter 5

What the Self Seeks

The signs on the Ascendant/Descendant offer information regarding how each individual approaches a partnership.

Aries Ascendant/Libra seventh
Libra Ascendant/Aries seventh

Mars rules fiery Aries, and Venus rules airy Libra.

Libra balance steadies Aries eagerness and helps to channel energy. Although Aries is independent in nature, partnership gives value to purpose for Aries.

Aries on the seventh house cusp stimulates a constantly new, fast-moving scene in associations, while at the same time having oneness of attraction, which brings both interest and stability to Libra.

This polarity needs energetic affection with reasonable physical expression.

Taurus Ascendant/Scorpio seventh
Scorpio Ascendant/Taurus seventh

Taurus, having material strength, seeks a supplement through Scorpio's physical strength. Easy living Taurus is stimulated by the Scorpio urgency to survive. Materialistic Taurus is complimented by the quiet emotions of Scorpio's courage.

Scorpio's physical expression of energy gains value when shared in love. The Taurus love nature tempers that deep drive with practical comforts of life, converting exertion into a lullaby.

Mars and Pluto rule watery Scorpio, and Venus rules earthy Taurus.

This polarity seeks an emotional outlet and physical exercise in comfortable surroundings.

Gemini Ascendant/Sagittarius seventh
Sagittarius Ascendant/Gemini seventh

Never-be-bored Gemini finds a sea of knowledge in the educated Sagittarius type whose flare for abundance and bounty allow much to talk about, whether privately, on the phone or in any gathering.

A Sagittarius Ascendant finds humor and pleasure in the wit of Gemini and enjoys the freedom which comes as a result of Gemini's mental, rather than physical, expression.

Mercury rules Airy Gemini, and Jupiter rules fiery Sagittarius.

This polarity seeks intellectual trust along with mental freedom of self-expression.

Cancer Ascendant/Capricorn seventh
Capricorn Ascendant/Cancer seventh

Cancer insecurity stabilizes through the experience of Capricorn, knowing that companionship can be long lasting. Capricorn's business ability complements Cancer's sensitivity to the public, equaling success.

Serious Capricorn seeks the childlikeness of Cancer as a release from the major business of existing, and finds emotional expression in partnership.

Moon rules watery Cancer, and Saturn rules earthy Capricorn.

This polarity allows an exchange of identity as child-parent and parent-child, each wanting on occasion to fill the other's role.

Leo Ascendant/Aquarius seventh
Aquarius Ascendant/Leo seventh

Romantically possessive Leo seeks and attracts the unique, rare, one-of-a-kind to complement the royal throne. Leo knows the Aquarian type is endowed with "follow-ship."

Aquarius on the Ascendant seeks the cooperation of a regal Leo type, one of whom to be proud. Aquarius intuitively knows from whom love comes.

Sun rules fiery Leo, and Uranus rules airy Aquarius.

This polarity is a combination of self love versus universal love, and is blessed with endurance by its fixity, but can be endangered by jealousy and over-possessiveness.

Virgo Ascendant/Pisces seventh
Pisces Ascendant—Virgo seventh

Virgo, the tester, seeks and attracts the ideal, often going through life searching for the Holy Grail or, early in life, accepting the imperfect Pisces type only to try to remold it.

To Pisces, partnership is a total commitment, either as the ideal partner or as a game of mystery, playing games of evasion and illusion.

Mercury rules earthy Virgo, and Neptune rules watery Pisces.

This polarity swings on a pendulum between imagery and reality—"for better or worse."

Chapter 6

Sex

The eighth house of the chart describes attitudes toward sex and sexual ability. Love is the fifth house and physical expression of passion is the eighth house.

One individual may be very shy in courtship (fifth house) and brazen in sex (eighth house); another may be sporting and flirty in romance (fifth house), yet afraid of physical contact (eighth house). The important point is whether the other person's attitude fills the desires of your corresponding house.

Anyone who has a set sexual routine will not satisfy a partner who has Uranus in the eighth house or Aquarius on the eighth house cusp. Uranus and Aquarius require change and experimentation. An eighth house Uranus becomes bored with monotonous routine.

The eighth house also shows what the partner brings to the partnership in a material way. Most people know how others fit into their material plans, but we can learn that without the intimacy of sex.

There are givers and there are takers. Relationships work best with one of each with no regard as to which sex gives and which takes. It is the balance of give and take that is important.

A point to ponder: There are more divorces during times of prosperity than poverty. In poverty, people share, and sharing is a necessary ingredient for love.

Eighth House

The eighth house represents what one expects the mate to bring to the partnership, both materially and physically. It traditionally is called the house of sex. As such, sexual expression through desire is described by the eighth house, by any planet there and by the ruler of the house with its aspects.

Planetary influence is not considered here; only the type is considered, as indicated by the sign on the cusp. The type will be attracted regardless of whether it is beneficial or not. The ruling planets will describe how the attraction develops and the individual deals with the energy and chooses positive or negative results.

To explain: A loaded eighth house may belong to a celibate who has spent many years leading a crusade concerning birth control or abortion.

Aries on the eighth house cusp (Virgo Ascendant) expects the partner to be financially independent and put forth energy toward joint income. Sexual desires are impulsive, fiery, energetic and of short duration.

Taurus on the eighth house cusp (Libra Ascendant) expects the partner to bring to the union material values and beautiful things that enhance luxury. Sexual desires are based on love or love of money. The expression is slow paced, relaxed and in a "pink satin sheets" atmosphere.

Gemini on the eighth house cusp (Scorpio Ascendant) expects the partner to bring two sources of income for joint partnership. Sexual desires are mentally stimulated and, because of the mental intensity, a repeat of the sex act is often required for total satisfaction.

Cancer on the eighth house cusp (Sagittarius Ascendant) expects the partner to bring nothing in particular in the way of material things—well, maybe a family owned business—and might move into the home already established by the partner.

Sexual impulses fluctuate and are based on emotions. Anything that touches the emotional nature disrupts the sex act.

Leo on the eighth house cusp (Capricorn Ascendant) expects a royal dowry via the mate. Preferably, both the personal reputation and bank account would be honorable and impressive. Sexual impulses have a flair for the dramatic, a stage show with Leo the director. Quality sets the scale rather than quantity.

Virgo on the eighth house cusp (Aquarius Ascendant) expects the partnership to produce order, purity in values (no stolen property) and devotion. The immoral Virgo reverses all these things. Sexual service is rendered only to one who, after close inspection, qualifies as meeting the requirements of their inner feelings. Virgo on the eighth is very particular about the mixing of Moon, Venus, Mars and Pluto. No venereal diseases, please.

Libra on the eighth house cusp (Pisces Ascendant) expects the partner to bring a guitar, a piano, an orchestra, even a radio—just say it with music. Bring beauty to the scene, whether for work or play. Sex is for the pleasure of expressing love. No hurt feelings or unforgiving attitudes can survive in the Libra eighth house.

Scorpio on the eighth house cusp (Aries Ascendant) expects the partner to bring more than appears on the surface, such as a hidden treasure or a birthright to an inheritance. Because of the deep-seated emotions of Scorpio, sexual desires may be so suppressed that they erupt when control is over-extended, appearing to be impulsive.

Sagittarius on the eighth house cusp (Taurus Ascendant) expects the partner to bring to the union much of whatever it is, so long as it is valuable or adds to comfort and no debts are included. A pocket full of credit cards acceptable. Sexual expression is ritualistic, generous and playful. Sagittarius is the sign of the big sport.

Capricorn on the eighth house cusp (Gemini Ascendant) expects the partner to bring success and prestige, or evidence in that direction. The sexual expression is "Now that we have made up our minds, let's get down to business."

Aquarius on the eighth house cusp (Cancer Ascendant) brings many things and expects the partner to bring to the union all sorts of ideas and possessions which can be useful to all concerned.

Sexual expression is friendly and sudden, yet long lasting. Arousal is emotionally stimulated through intuitive exchange of love.

Pisces on the eighth house cusp (Leo Ascendant) expects the partner to bring to the union the ability to understand and adore. Materially, Pisces looks for unknown wealth, such as a hide-away cabin or a cottage by the sea. The sexual expression seeks idealism with total commitment from the partner who is willing to forfeit identity and follow the leader of the act.

Chapter 7

Friendship

An ideal companion must be a friend. The eleventh house represents friendship which, otherwise stated, is returned love, because it opposes the fifth of love given.

A poem by Roy Croft says, "I love you not only for what you are but for what I am when I am with you." Anyone who can fulfill that blueprint is a good applicant for an ideal companion. What type person would that be?

Remember that everyone you know will fit differently into your horoscope than into the horoscope of another person. The cusp of your eleventh house will provide clues as to the types of people you attract as friends, and any planets in that house will furnish more details for description.

If anyone has difficulty with another person, whether lover, spouse, friend or another associate, the encounter with that individual affords an opportunity to learn to cope or deal with the circumstances that individual presents. What on the surface is a problem might develop into character-building events. It is unnatural for us to wish for such experiences, but when certain persons mean a great deal, we endeavor to tolerate the undesirable emotional conflicts.

The difficulty with afflictions to the eleventh house is that love is given to those who do not fully appreciate it; therefore, love and love returned is out of balance.

Chapter 8

Mars

Mars in one chart and how it fits in another person's chart can indicate a smooth supportive relationship or an irritating one.

Mars in either chart square Venus in the other is physically and sexually attracted, but there is friction because expressions of love and sex are not harmonious.

When there is an opposition of Mars in one chart to Venus in the other, it is usually the Mars person who is the aggressor. The sexual relationship is compatible if Venus is not offended.

When Mars in one chart and Venus in the other are conjunct, there is a strong love bond for the Venus person and physical satisfaction for the Mars person.

When Mars in one chart is sextile or trine Venus in the other, there is harmony in sexual relations.

It has been found that these interpretations are more accurate when in aspect by sign. A square could have a wide orb in cardinal, fixed or mutable signs and be more accurate for interpretation than if it has a close orb but is out-of-sign.

Example: A planet at 2 Aries is widely square a planet at 15 Cancer. There is irritation between these people. There may be a physical attraction, but there is also irritation.

A planet at 2 Aries is an out-of-sign square to a planet at 28 Gemini. Even though it is an aspect of friction, air and fire signs are more compatible than fire and water. One would think the tight orb would be more irritating, but water puts out fire while fire cannot bum at all without air. Consequently, air creates less friction than water.

Each person has Mars and each person has Venus. Mars is energy and physical expression, and some astrologers say that Mars has nothing to do with sex. I do not agree with that theory; however, there is much evidence that Pluto represents passion and, especially, perversion. Mars indicates natural sexual activity, while Pluto is passion uncontrolled, forceful and, perhaps, violent.

Pluto-Venus contacts between two people can be a strong sexual bond. Pluto is extremely possessive of Venus. Venus is bound to Pluto and has great difficulty breaking away if Pluto becomes abusive.

Two people can have all aspects between their collective Venus, Mars, and Pluto in good aspect and still experience severe emotional strain if there is conflict from one Moon to the other Mars.

When there are adverse aspects between Moon and Mars, the Mars person either purposely or unknowingly manages to hurt Moon's feelings frequently. Then Moon cries or pouts and Mars gets angry or runs away from tenderness.

These aspects between companions should be avoided if the situation is to be ideal.

Even one's progressed Moon adversely aspecting the other's natal Mars may bring a separation or divorce. However, the awareness of the temporal nature of a progressed aspect can afford some relief during times of stress.

Chapter 9

Mercury

There are very few ideal relationships, but the more closely the cogs of the wheel in one chart fit with the cogs of the other wheel, the better the chances for survival of love and sex.

As a relationship continues, communication and talking things over become even more important. An adverse aspect between one's Mars and the other's Mercury is argumentative and, if the other's Mars and Mercury are also adverse, a mediator is a must from time to time. It may be very difficult to have any understanding in communication between the partners.

Lack of communication is the most frequent cause of breakdowns in relationships. Some cases may be self explanatory. A woman was asked how she and her husband could tolerate all their arguments. "Fifteen minutes behind a closed door with him and nothing else matters," was her reply.

She was thirty-nine when they married. The forty-one year union ended with her death. Their only child was born when she was fifty-two. Not every hour was perfect, but there was a strong bond between them.

This story tells you that there are more ways to communicate than talking.

Chapter 10

Nodes and Karma

When the Nodes in two charts are conjunct planets, it is said to be a karmic relationship.

Another person's planet conjunct your North Node indicates good coming to you from that person.

Another person's planet conjunct your South Node indicates ties from a past life through which you can learn lessons for soul growth—or you can pile on more karma.

When your North Node is conjunct another's:

Sun: They represent authority to you.

Moon: Emotional stability and a feeling of being part of the family.

Mercury: You learn from or because of the person.

Venus: You receive love and favors.

Mars: The person uses energy for you.

Jupiter: You gain optimism, material values and spiritual upliftment.

Saturn: You gain through experience and an exchange of services.

Uranus: This is a friend to you now.

Neptune: Your inspiration and listener.

Pluto: Great influence over you; could be sexual.

Ascendant: Compatibility. Brings you favor.

When your South Node is conjunct another's:

Sun: Was an authority over you in a past life. May be a parent now. You feel obligated.

Moon: Your mother or child in a past life. Stirs your emotions.

Mercury: Your brother or sister in a past life. Mentally stimulating, but draining. May make you nervous.

Venus: Someone you loved in a past life, lover, relative, or friend. You give.

Mars: Unfriendly in a past life, could have hurt you in some way. You exert energy for that one now.

Jupiter: They helped you in the past. Now it's your turn.

Saturn: Could have been your father in a past life. Your responsibility in some way.

Uranus: Amend from the past. Promotes change in your life, which is unwelcome.

Neptune: Don't believe everything they say. They may not be able to keep their promise.

Pluto: Could be an enemy.

Ascendant: Many lifetimes together. You work out Karma.

Chapter 11

Portrait of Your Ideal Companion

Look for your own Ascendant or Sun sign substituted for the Ascendant. Using Aries as the example we find that Leo is the fifth house ruler. Leo is the sign of romance. You will attract romantic people to romance you, or at least you will want to attract this type of person. The person might not be a Leo Sun, Moon or Ascendant but will be romantic, or ideally so.

As an Aries, you have Libra on the seventh house (Descendant), and prefer cooperative people as partners. Sexy Scorpio is on the eighth house cusp, so you like a sex partner who is responsive and forceful in sex.

Reading the brief story on the lines opposite fifth, seventh and eighth, it says: "Aries prefers romantic Leo types for romance, cooperative Libra types as partners and the responsive sexuality of the of the Scorpio type."

Taurus says: "Taurus prefers someone who is like a servant in romance, a partner who can keep a confidence and devotion in the sex act.."

For more details refer to the pages about each sign under the chapter on each house previously listed.

If you have an interception, you can untangle some complexities in your own understanding of self by using the formula and reading not only the house cusps but from the Sun sign as if it were the Ascendant.

Aries	Fifth Leo	Romantic
Ascendant	Seventh Libra	cooperation and
Seeks	Eighth Scorpio	responsive sexuality.

The partner should love children, be willing to cooperate when needed, materially or mentally, and be emotionally prepared for emergencies.

***

Taurus	Fifth Virgo	Service,
Ascendant	Seventh Scorpio	confidential assistance,
Seeks	Eighth Sagittarius	and devotion.

The partner should be willing to set goals and calmly and determinedly work together toward reaching them.

***

Gemini	Fifth Libra	A pleasant, sociable
Ascendant	Seventh Sagittarius	and philosophical
Seeks	Eighth Capricorn	relationship with
		reasonable and pur-
		poseful expression
		of affection.
		Platonic?

The partner should be well educated, cultured and worthy of honorable recognition.

| Cancer Ascendant Seeks | Fifth Scorpio Seventh Capricorn Eighth Aquarius | Physical expression in a durable partnership with variable and interesting intimacy. |

The partner should be thoughtful and security conscious with a joint interest in home and business.

***

| Leo Ascendant Seeks | Fifth Sagittarius Seventh Aquarius Eighth Pisces | A glamorous courtship, a quick marriage and a submissive sex partner. |

The partner should always be ready for social gala among all sorts of people and forget it all for those private times alone.

***

| Virgo Ascendant Seeks | Fifth Capricorn Seventh Pisces Eighth Aries | One who can pass the tests and under stands the urgency of making many bank deposits. |

The partner should be willing to accept correction, enjoy inexpensive pleasures and be sexually responsive upon command.

***

| Libra Ascendant Seeks | Fifth Aquarius Seventh Aries Eighth Taurus | A friend on the horizon looking for love and peace. |

The partner should be sociable, ready to accept a challenge which will result in material wealth.

***

Scorpio	Fifth Pisces	Compassionate ro-
Ascendant	Seventh Taurus	mance, long lasting
Seeks	Eighth Gemini	love, and joint pos-
		sessions.

The partner should be understanding and able to know what Scorpio feels, but not mention it. Marriage is forever. Is there a willingness to make two trips to the bedroom for every one to the table?

***

Sagittarius	Fifth Aries	Impulsive romance
Ascendant	Seventh Gemini	with an intellectual
Seeks	Eighth Cancer	who is financially se-
		cure.

The partner should be willing to stand alone while Sagittarius is out gathering more higher mind wisdom, and be totally enthusiastic over the returning report.

***

Capricorn	Fifth Taurus	A loving romance
Ascendant	Seventh Cancer	with a security
Seeks	Eighth Leo	minded one who can
		sleep alone.

The partner must be willing to allow Capricorn to devote whatever time is necessary to build a substantial retirement fund.

***

Aquarius	Fifth Gemini	Mental entertainment
Ascendant	Seventh Leo	with a loving partner
Seeks	Eighth Virgo	who is very earthy.

The partner must be friendship oriented without discrimination but loyal to the one and only one Aquarian in the private partnership—until . . . Question

***

Pisces	Fifth Cancer	A domestic romance;
Ascendant	Seventh Virgo	one who serves home;
Seeks	Eighth Libra	cooking by candle-light with music.

The partner must be willing to splurge, at least occasionally, on elegant dining and dancing; when things don't go well, look for the message "Gone Fishing."

Chapter 12

Love, Like and Lust

Love comes from the fifth house of the horoscope, like comes from the seventh and lust comes from the eighth.

Very few couples have a high rating in all three levels. It is not likely that karma would be involved between the two if the rate is high. The lessons of life do not come that easily.

We evaluate all three levels of each person. One may find all three needs in an individual while the object of his or her affection only wants the body. Then there are those relationships where one loves and lusts and the other only likes. Then, God bless the reasoning powers of the lonely soul who loves, likes and lusts one who only wants money.

This is a complicated subject. There may never be a resolution between two people, but remembering the golden rule is the best way to survive and get the best out of any relationship until the karma is over when you can move on to the next stage of life. What is the golden rule? "Do unto others as you would have them do unto you."

If in a relationship two of the energies are favorable, a very good life can be enjoyed together. If a relationship is anchored by only one of the energies, it can get difficult. This level can be extremely satisfying if both people are in tune with the same levels. Let's say they have their own daytime lives and spend the romantic love times and sex times fully enjoying each other. They love together. Even then there is the danger of controversy over joint possessions, an eighth house issue. The great danger from the fifth house is jealousy.

Now consider love and like. In this instance one or both more than likely would have sexual deficiencies. One example is when a loving, nurturing type person whose body is more alive from the waist up than below the belt falls in love with one who is actually paralyzed. There would be very little sexual activity, if any, but they could be very happy together.

Like and lust present a totally different picture. So long as there is loyalty in lust, these two can spend an eternity together because they do not need to struggle with the possessive love that is threatened by jealousy, provided joint possessions are no issue.

If you have only one strong point, and it is love, you will give until it hurts—your patience, your time, your body, all of you.

If the only strong point is like, don't push it, but enjoy it as an acquaintance. This can be the easiest of all for emotional stability. Did you ever hear of anyone committing suicide or homicide over a person he or she likes?

44

If the only strong point is lust, spend the night together and don't get involved with the emotional pain. Sexual abuse is one of the greatest destroyers of all time.

Whatever the situation, understanding it astrologically from the perspective of both charts can mold a smooth relationship to its best advantage.

For the best of all things in love, love yourself and like who you are. But it can be a lonely life if you lust after self. Did you know that the same energy used in sex is the ultimate high on a spiritual plane? You don't have to eliminate sex—elevate it!

Spirituality is like advertising: It doesn't cost, it pays!

Chapter 13

Marriage and Divorce

One of the major assignments of an astrologer many centuries ago was to set nine fortunate dates and times for the wedding ceremony of the prince or princess of regal destiny. The influence of the husband and wife was important to the kingdom but perhaps more important was whether there would be heirs to the throne and how much financial and economic assistance would be brought to the nation.

The time of the ceremony is important to any wedding and serves as a birth chart for the life of the marriage. Information contained in this booklet has been compiled from legal records covering marriages lasting as many as forty years and as short as annulment.

The purpose of this book is to acquaint the student and professional with the potential difficulties as shown in the marriage, allowing an opportunity to ease tension and to cope with obstructions, in addition to enlightening the marriage partners on the path of happiness. It provides preparation time for the better developments in the marriage for promoting expansion in love, home, finances and relationships with each other and the children of the union.

The wedding chart reveals all aspects of the life of the couple and deserves the blessings of all interested persons.

It is suggested that the natal charts of the partners be compared to the marriage chart for clarification of such things as residential changes, birth of children and change in social activity or public image of the family.

Chapter 14

The Wedding Chart

The birth of the marriage is the time of the wedding ceremony and an exact chart would be when the couple is pronounced husband and wife.

The wedding chart is constructed just as any other birth chart but is not interpreted in the same way. Marriages have various beginnings and endings. Uranus will show where the urgency existed on the day of the ceremony. Was the wife anxious or was it the husband? Was there another urgency such as a pregnancy or need for joint finances? Did one of them need an immediate change of residence? Was the wedding a sudden decision or a long term engagement being culminated?

Progressions are applicable to the wedding chart just as they are to a birth chart and will also vibrate to the solar return. Any method of progressions which is workable is applicable.

A wedding is the birth of a partnership and therefore represents two people as individuals. The first house represents the husband and what he brings into the marriage, and the seventh house represents the wife and what she brings into the marriage, unless she made the proposal. Then the reverse applies, she first, he seventh.

The husband's financial support is shown by the second house of the chart and the eighth house the wife's contribution. Be sure to consider the attitudes toward their joint possessions and their spending habits, according to the interpretations of the second and eighth houses, analyzing the influence of the signs on the cusps and planets within the sign and the planet ruling the cusps.

Communication of the individuals is shown by the third and ninth houses of the chart. Husbands are described individually by the third and wives by the ninth. Religious philosophy of the family is shown by the ninth house, while the third shows the personal philosophy of the wife because it is her ninth house. Children's religious philosophy is shown by the first house, being the ninth from the fifth. However, each child is described by the houses of the chart, later expounded, and individual religion is more intricately detailed by alternate houses. That is, the first house of the chart is the ninth from the fifth, the third is the ninth from the seventh (second child's religion), the fifth is the ninth from the ninth (third child's religion), giving each child individuality; no two children are the same.

The husband's conversation (third house) and the wife's teaching (ninth house) blend to make the religious philosophy of the family. The father (husband) becomes the personal example to the first child since the first house describes the husband and the religion of the first child.

The ninth house describes the officiating clerk of the ceremony, whether it is an elaborate church wedding or a small public office chamber of an elected public authority delegated to perform weddings. Some very interesting wedding charts are made on the scene of hospital rooms, on board ships, and in emergency circumstances.

Wedding scenes are described by the tenth house of the chart, although the ninth house is the minister, judge, etc. The tenth house also describes the family which will be created by the union.

It has been found that sometimes the fourth house describes the scene, depending upon which family was more prominent for the occasion.

The fourth house describes the family of the husband and the home provided to the wedding couple. It also describes any hidden problems associated with the children resulting from the union, being the twelfth from the fifth. Because the fourth is the tenth from the seventh, it tells of the wife's public image created by the marriage.

Children are shown by the fifth and step-children are shown by the eleventh. The fifth house also shows how the family will be entertained and how they will vacation. The eleventh house shows the social life of the family and any creative talents of the wife. If the wedding chart describes a family-owned business, the business income is depicted by the eleventh house since it is the second from the tenth.

The twelfth house gives light to the hidden thoughts, secrets and potential confinements of the husband, and the sixth house describes the health and work of the husband. The houses are reversed for the wife. The sixth house also shows daily routine.

Wherever the Sun finds its place in the wedding chart shows the ego of the marriage, depending upon the sign and house of its location. If a wedding takes place with the Sun in the tenth house, the family will be prominent in some area. The Sun in the fifth house may find the family active in sports. Sun in the fourth house will keep the family at home. They may be active hosts, but at home.

The first house may not always represent the male, but may reflect the female, in which case it will be discovered that the female was the aggressor in the relationship or that she proposed the marriage.

Something needs to be said about homosexual relationships as married and about live-ins. It is practically impossible to set a "marriage" chart for a live-in relationship. The time of the dedication ceremony for homosexuals serves as the wedding chart the same as for male/female unions.

When the female energy is represented by the first house, it will be found that she is more the public figure or that they are supported by outside sources through her contacts, such as family inheritance.

Chapter 15

Danger Signals in the Wedding Chart

After studying many wedding charts which ended in divorce, it was discovered that there were some common danger signals. In most of the studies at least two of those signals were present.

Marriages are subject to troublesome times under the cycle of Saturn, just as are individuals. The third year is critical because Saturn is then fifteen degrees from its position at the time of the wedding, and from there the years are: seven, twenty-one, twenty-eight, thirty-five, forty-two and so on as long as the marriage lasts.

The progressed Moon operates on approximately the same cycle as Saturn. They are usually in different signs and different houses (the exception is the chart with a natal conjunction). So it behooves us to watch carefully that Moon and

Saturn do not severely afflict in the marriage chart so not to multiply trouble.

The early days of the marriage may suffer when the progressed Moon enters the next sign, and this can be any time during the first twenty-eight months of the marriage, depending upon the degree of the Moon at the time of the wedding.

All love relationships are in danger when Venus is retrograde, regardless of its direction in the wedding chart. Venus retrograde is falling out of love and takes on a Mars attitude, causing each partner to expect more of the other and each partner to be more individualistic.

When the Sun transits Aquarius, divorce rates rise. Aquarius is the sign of freedom, and Uranus rules divorce. Usually one of the parties does not want the divorce, but more often finds that the suddenness of it was the cause of the suffering and that the situation actually is better than before in some way.

Contrary to common belief, retrograde Mercury is not a guarantee of divorce. There will be changes in the marriage on the years Mercury progresses direct and, if divorce occurs, it may well coincide with Mercury returning by progression to the degree where it was in the wedding chart. Also, if Mercury is retrograde in the wedding chart and divorce does occur, the divorce will most likely be filed during a period when Mercury is transiting retrograde. If there is a secret marriage followed by a public ceremony, the chart of the public ceremony probably will have Mercury retrograde.

Mercury in the wedding chart represents the children born to the union, and a retrograde, if in the fifth, seventh, ninth, eleventh, etc. house, will depict that the pregnancy representing that child will result in a miscarriage. Now to clarify: The fifth house is the first child, the seventh house is the second child and the third child is the ninth house. If Mercury is retrograde in any of these houses, the child represented by that house will deliver prematurely, in which case the following alternate house will rule any next child to be born.

The anaretic degree of any sign is to be avoided in a wedding chart, especially for the degree of the Ascendant, Midheaven, Sun, Moon, Venus, Mars and Jupiter. This is said to be the degree of tears. The Ascendant is the marriage chart event and may be performed under tearful circumstances of someone. The Midheaven brings scandal or trouble from the parents.

Sun is the masculine image and authority of the chart and the twenty-ninth degree of the Sun destroys the identity of one of the parties. Moon in the twenty-ninth degree brings much unhappiness to the wife. Home and family may also suffer in time.

Venus influences happiness and love. Venus at the twenty-ninth degree denies love to one of the partners. Example: Early death of one of the partners or accident or illness immobilizing one.

Mars is vitality and energy. One of the partners will feel too restricted and the partnership may even be interspersed with actual combat. Venus and Mars at the twenty-ninth degree will have a bearing on the sexual relationship between the parties.

Jupiter represents the legality of the act and the ceremony itself. Jupiter in the twenty-ninth degree or retrograde in any degree is a threat to any marriage. Jupiter is just within the law. Did one lie about age?

One of the above mentioned planets in the twenty-ninth degree was evident in practically every chart examined in this research. Those charts not having a planet in the twenty-ninth degree had the Moon so near that it was strongly suspected that since those particular charts were for an unknown time, that the Moon could have been in the twenty-ninth degree. Also, the progressed Moon to that degree was prominent at the time of the divorce.

Uranus square Moon, Venus or Mars should be avoided in any wedding chart because Uranus is freedom and the square stimulates too much friction between the parties.

Three degree orbs were used for this study.

Chapter 16

Kennedy Wedding

In the wedding chart of Joan and Ted Kennedy, the Sun is in the tenth house in Sagittarius and Leo is on the seventh house cusp. The family is prominent, and he is known for his legal knowledge, represented by both Sagittarius and the seventh house.

It is also interesting that 26 Scorpio occupies the cusp of the tenth house, and the family was brought strongly to the public because of incidents in connection with death. Scorpio rules death.

The rulers of both the fourth and tenth houses are located in the tenth house, showing them to come from not one but two well-known families. The Moon is in the sixth house, which is her twelfth. Children cause confinement for her but were her secret reason for marriage. She wanted children. Her love of children is obvious by the seventh house being ruled by Leo. The ruler of the first house represents him and,

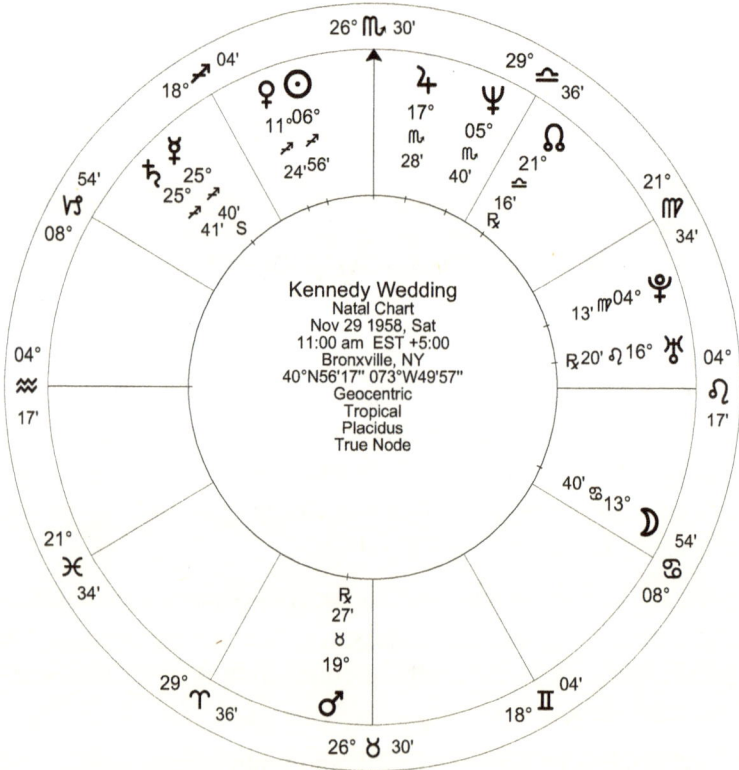

Kennedy Wedding
Natal Chart
Nov 29 1958, Sat
11:00 am EST +5:00
Bronxville, NY
40°N56'17" 073°W49'57"
Geocentric
Tropical
Placidus
True Node

being placed in the seventh, tells us she is under his dominion. The Sun ruling her is trine Uranus, showing that they are compatible in a friendly, unique way even as husband and wife. Uranus is square Jupiter (the ceremony) but Jupiter is trine Moon, and Uranus is trine Sun, which is an out for problems.

Pluto ruling the tenth is in the seventh house, indicating that public events relating to the family fall squarely in her lap. Mars is the co-ruler of the tenth and is retrograde in the third of communications, bringing him repeatedly into the news. Mars also rules the third house whose cusp is at twenty-nine degrees.

The ninth house of world news has Jupiter and Neptune in Scorpio, deepening the nature of the news issues and reaching a wide scope. Neptune places some doubt in the veracity of all that may be said on some scores. Ninth house holding Jupiter and Neptune tell us that the family is of a spiritual and philosophical nature.

The Moon of any wedding chart describes the daily events in the life of the marriage. The Kennedy wedding chart has Moon in Cancer in her twelfth. This is her confinement because of children (Moon) and his service to the people (his sixth house). Since he is represented by the first house and the Moon describes his health, we know that he suffers from upset stomach frequently because of emotions because Moon is inconjunct Venus, the planet of social functions and overindulgence.

His income is shown by the second house ruled by Neptune in the ninth, being the voice of others (third from the seventh), and it is meaningful that her income is shown by the ruler of the eighth, her second, being Mercury located in the eleventh, her fifth. She is paid for having and caring for children.

Mercury's placement tells about the children. In the Kennedy chart we find Mercury in the bountiful sign of Sagittarius and in the eleventh house of social affairs. Mercury is conjunct Saturn, representing tradition, and not far past Venus in the same sign. Venus rules the fourth house of the home. binding the children in a close family relationship. Mercury is sextile Jupiter and Neptune in the third, the Mother's word meaning they honor her, but since her ruler, the Sun, falls in their twelfth of secret sorrows, they pity her.

Venus describes happiness of the marriage. In the Kennedy chart, Venus is in the tenth house and trine the first house ruler, Uranus, located in her first house (seventh house of the chart). Venus is conjunct the Sun, ruler of the seventh house, representing her. There is a natural yod formed by inconjuncts to Moon in Cancer and Mars retrograde in Taurus in the third and sixth. The yod events relate to the children and bad news or false information broadcast concerning the family.

The Nodes are found in the second and eighth houses; Aries is in the second, ruled by Pisces, and Libra is in the eighth, ruled by Virgo. The purpose of ths marriage is to learn about give-and-take in partnership. Pisces and Virgo on the cusps say service and understanding are a part of the purpose. Second and eighth houses provide opportunity for soul growth concerning joint possessions/morality.

In the final analysis we would have to suspect that Joan rules the hone and the family and allows him enough freedom to let him be happy.

Kennedy Split

Review of the Kennedy divorce and some of the events lending up to divorce has provided the astrologer with more information concerning the wedding event.

The Moon of the chart is in the critical twelfth degree of Cancer, warning that there would be many times when the family would be faced with emotional stress. In 1978, when Joan moved out into an apartment, the progressed Moon squared that critical degree in Aries (need to be alone). Jupiter was in the same degree of the Nodes by progression at the same time. Karma of the legality had served them.

Progressed Sun was conjunct progressed Saturn and had been in orb for three years. Through this progression of Sun to Saturn, another warning signal becomes brighter. In the wedding chart, Saturn is conjunct Mercury. Mercury progressed retrograde the second year of marriage, and progressed direct in 1979. When she took the apartment in Boston, they were not publically considering it a separation. She was withdrawing from alcohol and reinstating her education in music. Neptune rules alcohol, and we find Neptune in her third house of the wedding chart—her way to communicate.

In 1979, Mars progressed direct at 16 Taurus square Uranus in the seventh (her). Conversation and communication between them that had been held back came out in the open; at the same time, she demanded freedom of self. Progressed Mars was opposing Jupiter (houses three and nine), adding more fuel to the communication fire. Note that these houses have twenty-nine degrees on the cusps. The interpretation for twenty-nine degrees is "can't get enough," either because of not being available or it taking much to satisfy.

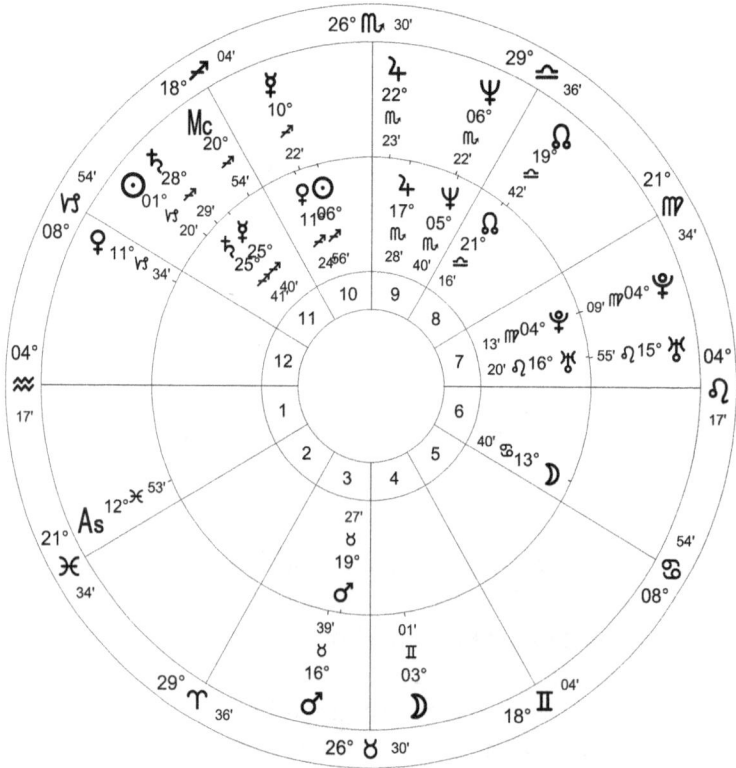

Uranus ground hard into 29 Scorpio three times by transit in 1981, and Joan and Ted announced their full intentions to end their marriage early in the year and spent much of that year planning and arranging their circumstances in order to make a fair and congenial dissolution of their marriage.

Progressed Sun had just come through 29 Sagittarius and was entered Capricorn when the announcement was made of their intent to divorce. Divorce was filed and granted in December 1982, with transiting Pluto conjunct the twenty-nine degree ninth house cusp of legality of the wedding chart.

Maybe that Moon in a critical degree deserves more attention.

Critical Degrees
Cardinal signs: 0, 13, 26
Fixed signs: 9, 21
Mutable signs: 4, 17

Note: Average daily notion of the Moon is thirteen degrees per day. Begin with zero degrees of cardinal signs and keep adding thirteen degrees.

Chapter 17

Culmination of Marriage

The parties in the example in this chapter are unidentified for confidentiality; however the records are printed with permission. Charts included are those of the wedding, filing for divorce, and the dissolution of the marriage event.

The danger signals in the wedding chart consist of Sun at 29 Sagittarius, Moon at 29 Libra and Jupiter opposition Uranus.

The twenty-ninth degree implies "can't get enough." Sun at 29 Sagittarius is in the tenth house of career. His work took him far and wide weekly. Moon at 29 Libra, the partnership, in the first house and intercepted left her at home when he would have been frequently allowed to have her accompany him. The result was that she couldn't get enough partnership and sought companionship elsewhere. He couldn't get enough travel and work.

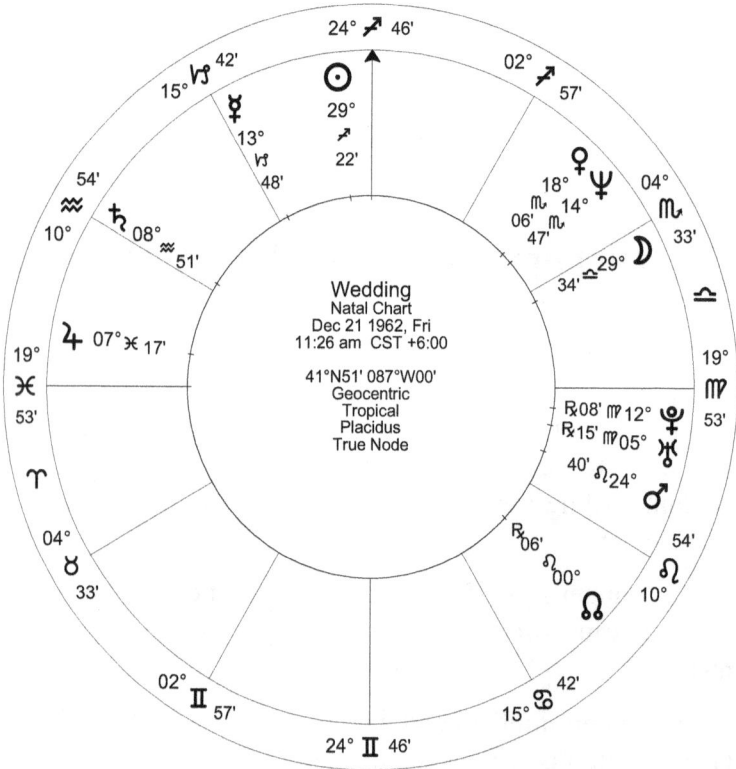

Wedding
Natal Chart
Dec 21 1962, Fri
11:26 am CST +6:00

41°N51' 087°W00'
Geocentric
Tropical
Placidus
True Node

Remember that when there is too much, it is because something has not been brought to rest. He could have asked for local work in the same company and been granted it, but he couldn't get enough. One person with Venus in Capricorn in the twenty-ninth degree says the rule doesn't apply and that she has plenty of work. Then why does she still advertise?

Intercepted signs in the first and seventh indicate complex self-identity or loss of identity of both parties. Mars and Venus rule those signs and are in square aspect. Mars is in her twelfth house; she feared him and was strongly overshadowed by him when they were in public or a social situation. Mars trines the Midheaven.

How did he lose his identity? Pisces is the Ascendent ruler, with Neptune in the eighth house of the chart. The first four years of the marriage she worked to assist him in getting his doctorate. Neptune is in her second house. She was the family bookkeeper. It continued to operate as long as the marriage lasted, one way or another. Later they each had their own allowance and neither made any effort to know how the other used his or her share.

Gemini and Sagittarius are the double signs on the third and fourth houses and on the ninth and tenth houses. These houses represent their home, his home, her work (fourth); and her home, his work (tenth). Communication is the third and ninth houses, and Mercury is ruler of the third and fourth and is in a critical degree of Capricorn in the fourth house of the home, and Jupiter is ruler of ninth and tenth and is buried in the twelfth of the chart, her sixth.

She had a deep desire to be productive and work (Jupiter in her sixth of work), but he objected while she complied

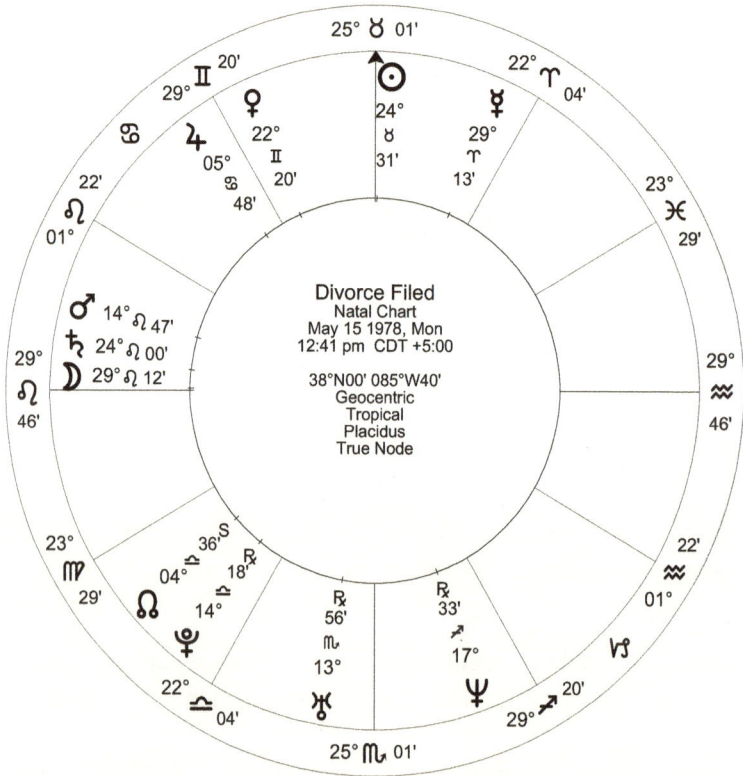

Divorce Filed
Natal Chart
May 15 1978, Mon
12:41 pm CDT +5:00

38°N00' 085°W40'
Geocentric
Tropical
Placidus
True Node

since Moon rules their children and is intercepted in the seventh house. She stayed home with the children and for him after she helped him get through school.

The Nodes are in the fifth and eleventh houses. The children obviously were the karma of the marriage. The signs Leo and Aquarius represent ego and individuality. It is certain that both learned much through the relationship.

On the date she filed for divorce, transiting Jupiter was at 3 Cancer intercepted in the eleventh house T-square the Nodes in Libra/Aries. Saturn, ruling the other intercepted sign, was conjunct Mars of the wedding chart and square Midheaven and transiting Sun in Taurus. A Mars-Saturn conjunction is like driving with brakes on, going nowhere with a struggle. Saturn in Leo equals restricted love and romance.

His ruler of the marriage chart, Neptune, is now in a critical degree in the fourth house and rules the eighth of the filing chart. Remember that Neptune represents him in the wedding chart. His complex identity emerges. He took all joint funds and transferred them to a third person, which left only the home equity to be divided between them.

Keep in mind that one does not dictate the time that an attorney files anything. Now look at the twenty-nine degree points. Moon at 29 Leo conjunct the 29 Leo Ascendant and 29 Aquarius on the seventh house. Do you recall their need to be self expressive and individualistic? Leo/Aquarius can't get enough ego and individuality, or romance and freedom, as you please. Moon was at 29 Libra in the wedding chart—can't get enough partnership and now in Leo love?

Mercury is at 29 Aries in the third of communications, can't get enough. The double house cusps were Leo/Aquar-

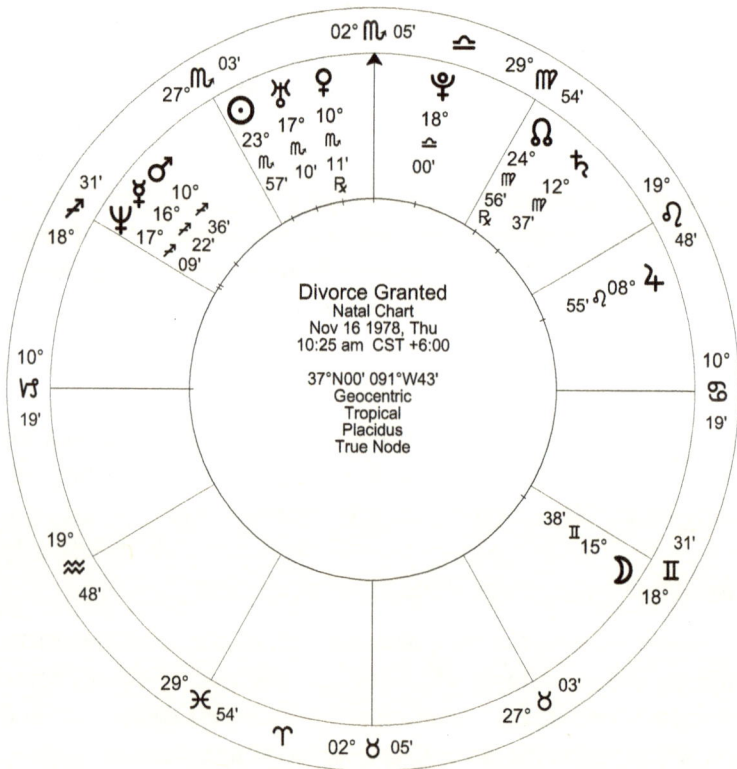

Divorce Granted
Natal Chart
Nov 16 1978, Thu
10:25 am CST +6:00

37°N00' 091°W43'
Geocentric
Tropical
Placidus
True Node

70

ius, twelfth house to both of them is separation. Houses five and eleven hold the twenty-ninth degree with the intercepted signs in those houses. Rulers were Moon and Saturn. Moon had just passed over Saturn, leaving a trail of sadness.

Progressed Moon was at 29 Taurus, the degree of tears and, although neither of them wanted a divorce, their differences were irreconcilable.

Six months passed before the divorce was granted. Jupiter, which rules legal action and the courts and judges, was intercepted in the filing chart, delaying the final hearing.

In the progressed chart at the time of the of the divorce, Venus was at 29 Scorpio square the filing chart Ascendant and at the midpoint between the twenty-nine degree Sun and Moon in the wedding chart. Progressed Moon opposed progressed Venus at the time of filing. Love was dead.

Progressed Midheaven was almost 10 Capricorn, just one degree off the Ascendant of the event of granting of the divorce. Progressed Midheaven was exactly conjunct wedding chart eighth house cusp. Transiting South Node (karma) of the granting chart was conjunct the eighth house cusp of the filing chart. The case was closed.

Transiting Moon at the moment of the granting was within thirty-seven minutes of progressed Moon at that time. The first aspect the Moon made after the culmination of the marriage and the granting of the divorce was a sextile to Jupiter. Freedom! The sign was Leo. Transiting Saturn was conjunct Pluto in the wedding chart, being the eighth house of the granting chart.

www.ingramcontent.com/pod-product-compliance
Lightning Source LLC
LaVergne TN
LVHW011412080426
835511LV00005B/490